PIRATES AHOY!

Pirate Kit

by Rosalyn Tucker

Consulting editor: Gail Saunders-Smith, PhD

raintree

a Capstone company — publishers for children

Raintree is an imprint of Capstone Global Library Limited, a company incorporated in England and Wales having its registered office at 7 Pilgrim Street, London, EC4V 6LB – Registered company number: 6695582

www.raintree.co.uk
myorders@raintree.co.uk

Text © Capstone Global Library Limited 2015
The moral rights of the proprietor have been asserted.

Editorial Credits
Michelle Hasselius, editor; Kazuko Collins, designer; Pam Mitsakos, media researcher; Gene Bentdahl, production specialist

ISBN 978 1 406 29351 7 (hardback)
19 18 17 16 15
10 9 8 7 6 5 4 3 2 1

ISBN 978 1 406 29356 2 (paperback)
20 19 18 17 16
10 9 8 7 6 5 4 3 2 1

British Library Cataloguing in Publication Data
A full catalogue record for this book is available from the British Library.

Photo Credits
Alamy: © Mary Evans Picture Library, 5, © Wim Wiskerke, 15; Bridgeman Images: Look and Learn, 11, 13, 17, cover; Mary Evans Picture Library: 19; Shutterstock: Dmitrijs Bindemanis, 21, Elenarts, 7, Eva Bidiuk (ship silhouette), cover, Triff, 9
Design Elements: Shutterstock: A-R-T (old paper), La Gorda (rope illustration), vovan (old wood)

Printed in China.

Contents

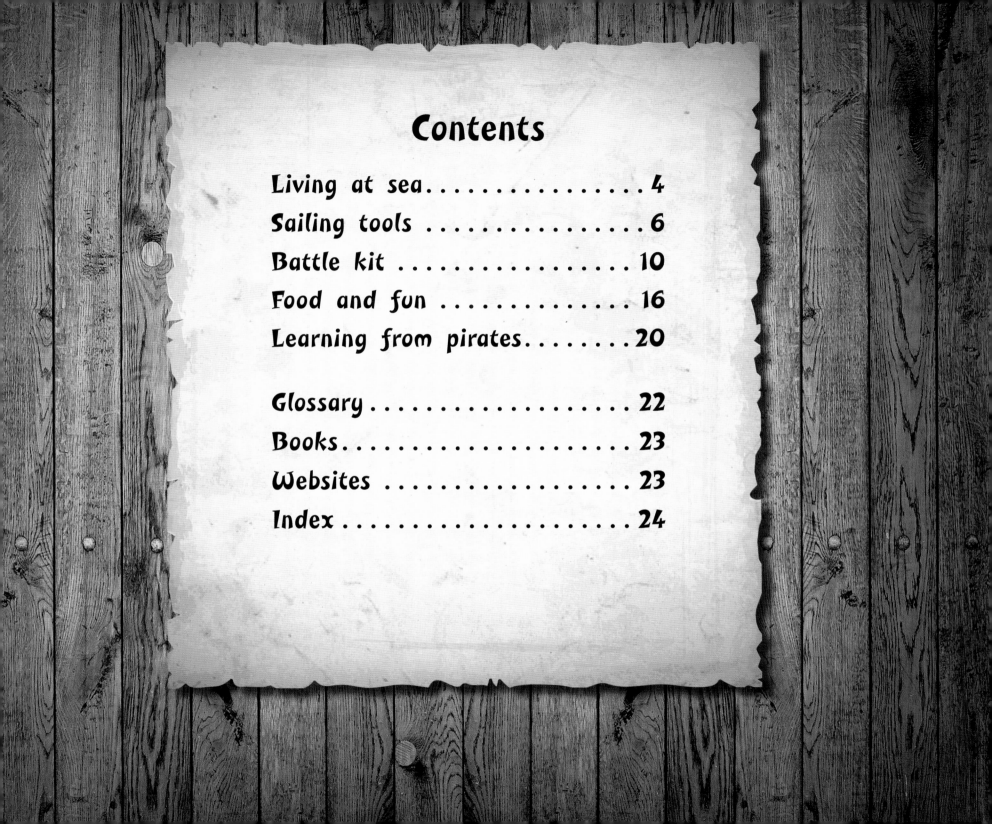

Living at sea

Pirates lived at sea during the
Golden Age of Piracy (1690–1730).
Pirates needed a lot of kit to
live and fight on pirate ships.

Pirates could spend months at sea.

Sailing tools

Sails were like engines for ships. Pirates raised sails high into the air on masts. The sails caught strong winds. The wind pushed the ships through the water.

sails

The more sails a ship had, the faster it could go.

Pirates needed special kit to guide their ships. They used maps, charts and compasses to find their way. Pirates often stole these items from other ships.

A compass helped a pirate sail in the right direction.

Battle kit

Pirates always had to be ready to
fight. Cannons were powerful weapons
on a ship. Pirates also fought with
short swords called cutlasses.

Large ships could carry more than 40 cannons.

Pirates threw stinkpots onto a ship before they attacked. Stinkpots were clay pots filled with smelly fish parts. Pirates wanted to make the ship's crew too ill to fight.

A ship's crew was easier to fight against after pirates threw stinkpots.

One of the most useful weapons
was a pirate's Jolly Roger flag.
Pirates painted skulls or bones
on their flags to scare other sailors.

a Jolly Roger flag

Food and fun

Pirates kept salted meats and drinking water on their ships. But sometimes they needed more food. Pirates caught fish. But they also stole fresh food from other ships.

Pirates could hunt for food when they were on land.

Sometimes pirates got bored at sea. They played music with drums and fiddles. Some pirates even had pets such as parrots or monkeys.

Pirates are often shown with parrots in books and paintings.

Learning from pirates

Charts, weapons and sails
were important kit for pirates.
We study these tools to learn
about pirate life. Pirate kit is
displayed in museums today.

Pirate kit can be found in museums around the world.

Glossary

cannon heavy gun that fires large metal balls

compass tool used for finding directions

cutlass short sword with a curved blade

display show something

engine machine that makes the power needed to move something

fiddle violin

Golden Age of Piracy period from 1690 to 1730, when thousands of people became pirates around the world

kit items needed for a job or an activity

mast tall pole on a ship's deck that holds its sails

pirate person who steals from ships and towns

Books

I Wonder Why Pirates Wore Earrings and Other Questions About Pirates, Pat Jacobs (Kingfisher, 2012)

Pirates (Legends of the Sea), Rebecca Rissman (Raintree, 2011)

Pirates (Secret World), Kay Barnham (Scholastic, 2009)

Websites

www.bbc.co.uk/cbeebies/swashbuckle-online/games
Find the treasure and make the pirates walk the plank!
Try these fun pirate games.

www.jerseyheritage.org/learning/teacher-resources-pirates
Follow the links to test your knowledge of pirate kit with
a pirate wordsearch!

Index